The BIG MISTAKE of SAUL

Authored by K.B. Ransford

Foreword by Bishop E.A.T Sackey

Edited by K. Lee

The Big Mistake of Saul

First edition published by Krystal Lee Enterprises (KLE Publishing)
ISBN: 978-1-945066-10-8
E-book: 978-1-945066-11-5

Second edition published by Texture Publishing (Pty) Ltd
ISBN: 978-1-77634-394-2
E-book: 978-1-77634-395-9

Edited by K. Lee

Printed and bound in South Africa

FOREWORD

A word from Bishop E.A.T Sackey

The Bible enjoins us not to frustrate the grace of God. Paul wrote and asked whether the grace bestowed on us should be in vain. The story of Saul is one of the most pathetic ones in the Bible. Saul sets out to go and look for his father's missing donkeys, however, God had a higher plan for him. At the end of a two day search without success we see the prophet Samuel anointing him as the first king of Israel. What a shock?

And truthfully, he did not feel qualified because he knew his tribe is the least in Israel and his family is the least in the tribe. But somehow God had overlooked all that and selected him. So what went wrong? That's the big question! What is it that has the potential of messing up God's undeserved favor He bestows on us? Indeed the blessing was supposed to be perpetuated to all of Saul's generation.

In this book Bishop Ransford painstakingly takes us through the processes that made Saul slip from the place of grace to disgrace and humiliation. It is both sad and scary. The ultimate reason for his success is the presence of God and therefore the ultimate reason for his demise was when he lost the presence of God. Dear reader, take time and laboriously read through the pages of this book.

You will discover that it is not the so called

'big sins' that brought him low, but sins like pride, disobedience, fear, and many more simpler ones. Do not put the book down. Study it and let it instruct, guide and bless you.

Bishop, thank you for challenging us not to 'miss the mark' of His presence.

BISHOP E.A.T. SACKEY

SENIOR ASSOCIATE,

LIGHTHOUSE CHAPEL INTERNATIONAL

TABLE OF CONTENTS

INTRODUCTION

An Introduction to the Big Mistake of Saul

As years go by the stability, the determination of our Salvation in Christ and our intent on sharing the Gospel with the nations should be at an all-time high. Christians believe we are living in the last days. In fact, we have been living in the last days since the death and resurrection of Christ. Today there is an imperative mandate pertaining to operating in the specific gifting and calling that God has placed upon our lives.

Each and every child of God has a gift and a

calling over their life that they ought to answer. Why? Because we are all held accountable to operate in our gifting for the glorification of Christ, to benefit the Saints, and to minister to the Lost, or reach mankind.

Where in the Bible does it say that we will be held accountable for the gifts we use or bury in the sand? In Matthew 25 the Bible gives the account of the talents or shekels. There were three persons; each person received a gift from the Lord. Each person had the same level of responsibility although the value, quantity, or talents differed. The Lord had the same expectations of the three, to return to Him a harvest, better known today as a return on investment (ROI).

In addition, we can understand that with God equality is not bestowing the same gifts and talents to each person, but having the same expectation. No matter who you are or the strength and limitations you may have, the Lord knows what you can and cannot handle. He will not put more on us than we can bear (1 Corinthians 10:13 KJV).

So, one person received one talent, another two talents, and the third five talents; and yet according to God he had the same expectation for the three. The Lord gives us gifts not so we can admire our talents, say how wonderful they are or look, not even how they can specifically bless you; but how they can bless the One who gave it to you. The talents could be physical things you can do such as singing, writing, playing an instrument, administration, preaching, teaching, speaking, and so forth. These gifts without the presence of God can be made to edify ourselves or we can create a ministry that is laced with the spirit of iniquity.

Iniquity, serving the Lord under false pretense;

saying you serve the Lord and are seeking His will, yet you are seeking your own agenda and chasing after your dreams. Keep in mind a scripture and a scenario that many people love to quote by Isaiah 6:8.

"Whom shall I send? And who will go for us?
And I said,
"Here am I. Send me!"

We must be careful and not forget that a commitment we make to the Lord is binding. If you say you are willing, don't be surprised if you are sent. When you are sent, be sure to complete the task at hand because your lack of obedience impacts others and many times we don't know by how much. The Lord is looking for the faithful, can you be— will you be counted?

Furthermore, to be counted available for service

by the Almighty God. The Lord is looking for a willing vessel that is not offering lip service but is sincere and trust the Lord with all their being. You must trust that the plans the Lord has for you is greater and a priority over your own. You have to be willing to follow the Lords instructions and maintain His course no matter the turbulence you face on the way. When you are faithful in following after the Lord's plan for your life, then you will move from Glory to Glory. Moving from Glory to Glory can only be accomplished when we are in the will of God.

The Lord has shown me that we can operate in a gift from the Lord but His presence be separated from us. We learn this through the life account of King Saul. He was operating as king even while the presence of the Lord had departed from him and rested on David; the new king. The possibility of operating in life without the Lord's presence may seem strange for a believer; but the Lord began to show me—and I felt burden to share with His people, how this can become so.

How can we avoid making the big mistakes of Saul? We must first never depart from the presence of God. This close-knit connection may appear a mystery, but through the reading of this book I intend to share how you too can maintain the presence of the Lord in your life!

When we are first converted, or give our lives to Christ, there is a feeling, an emotional high that is unexplainable that takes over our lives. We believe hard and we are completely convinced that everything in the Word is true. Nothing can overcome or cause us to leave this newly found relationship. It is easy to enjoy the divine presence of God, but then something happens.

It's nothing major but seemingly a small issue that comes up and challenges our belief. We are tested to think on if it is wrong to cheat on a test, on taxes, people. If we are not diligent over our beliefs, we can manipulate the Word by bending Truth to fit our agenda, a seemingly small compromise will cause a ripple effect in our lives.

This ripple effect can cause the presence of the Lord to leave your life, while you may remain unaware. It is dangerous to think, because the Lord has not appeared to judge you for your transgression that He agrees with them. Don't be deceived. We are all gifted with gifts, would you not agree?

Natural talents are gifts that are bestowed upon us that empower us to fulfill our destiny. Just like we are all gifted to have a trade or a way of employment, we are also gifted with spiritual gifts. In 1 Corinthians 12:4-11 it says in a nutshell:

"The Word of wisdom, the word of knowledge, faith, healing, miraculous powers, prophecy, distinguishing between spirits, speaking in tongues and the interpretation of tongues."

These are the spiritual gifts that the Lord Almighty gives to the body of believers for the edification of the Saints. There is a difference between praying in your prayer language and speaking in tongues. God shares a prayer language with all believers that functions as a divine language for communication between God and man. Speaking in tongues requires an interpreter, and if there is no interpreter, speaking in tongues should not be done before an audience because the masses cannot understand it (1 Corinthians 14:28).

How can you know or recognize when the presence of God has departed from your life if you are still able to speak in other utterance? How should you know when the power attached to the tongue's spoken is no longer there? Do not be deceived you can speak in tongues, do godly activities, and the presence—the power of God can be absent. We can have the form of godliness and the power of God be far from us (2 Timothy 3:5).

I believe strongly by the conviction of the Holy Spirit that God will open your eyes to see the mistakes of Saul. As well as learn how we can learn from his faults to improve our relationship with God and our lives overall. This book demonstrates a godly revelation, supported by scripture, for how and why the presence of God departed from Saul. And yes, how the same can happen to any of us if we are not mindful of the things of God. This book will outline signs and the evidence if the presence of God has departed from your life.

When you begin to come across these signs in

your life—or sense these things, take heed to the divine alarm that the presence of God is missing in your life. The good news, although the presence may have departed, there is hope for restoration. In this book, I talk about how the Lord may allow us to get back to where we have fallen.

Now, a precursor to the subject of this book, Saul was a character in the Bible that was no special case and too made mistakes as others. His mistakes are mistakes any of us can make and perhaps may have already made. Mistakes, choices, paths we take can result to the departure of the presence of God from our lives.

You may ask what is the presence of God? I believe the presence can best be explained as the divine Spirit of God that flows from the throne room of God, accompanied by gifting's and a calling on your life that helps you to execute a divine assignment, bestowed over one's life to accomplish its purpose; whether that be a kingship anointing, prophetic, teaching, preaching, serving, and etc.

All believers have access to the throne room of grace. When you are born again, your gifts in the spirit realm are quickened and heighten so that you may achieve God's purpose for your life. God chooses who He does for His purpose.

Your background, social, or economic standing bears no affect on what God calls for you to do.

You see Saul was a man of lowly means. In fact, he didn't live better than many of us and was of a simple mind. He didn't desire to become king and that didn't change God's plan for his life. The Bible says in 1 Samuel 9: 21

"Am I not a Benjaminite, from the least of the

tribes of Israel? And is not my clan the humblest of all the clans of the tribe of Benjamin? Why then have you spoken to me in this way?"

This humility is commonly found among new believers when they are engrafted into the body of Christ. Like with Saul, the Lord has ushered us to His table by a man or woman of God similar to how Samuel welcomed Saul. 1 Samuel 9:23,24 describes the welcome like this,

"…Bring the portion I gave you, of which I told to you, 'Put it aside. So the cook took up the leg and what was on it and set them before Saul. And Samuel said, "See, what was kept is set before you. Eat, because it was kept for you until the hour appointed, that you might eat with the guests."

What so ever the Lord has appointed and set aside for you to do in your life no man or demonic force in hell can take it from you. No one can take from the Lord or cancel His plans for you. Saul was the same. His problem was not what man could take from him, but what he would give way. Saul's life was protected as long as he walked in the calling and decrees from the Lord. His life took a terrible turn when the presence of God left out of his life and kingship.

I believe there is a lot a believer can learn from the account of Saul. The first is how we all discover our fist Love, The Lord. The second, is how we may all fall victim to the enemy and lose our divine rights as a child of God, as a result of the departed presence of God in our lives. Join me on this journey through the "Big Mistake of Saul" and learn to identify the signs and evidence for how God's presence departed from his life. His story can help all of us safeguard the Lord's presence in our lives, ministry, and calling.

THE DIVINE SEARCH

The Divine Search for the King

1 Samuel 9:3

"Now the donkeys of Kish, Saul's father, were lost. So Kish said to Saul his son, "Take one of the young men with you, and arise, go and look for the donkeys."

Saul's appointment with destiny first started with obedience. "Thou shall obey your father and mother" was God's instruction to man passed down by Moses to His people (Exodus 20:12). What we may not realize is following God's commandments gives rewards. To be used by God we have to understand obedience is greater than sacrifice (1 Samuel 15:22). When the Lord gives His orders it is not up to us to consider if we agree before obedience. The Lord does not error and it is true His ways are not ours because they are greater (Isaiah 55:8).

Have you realized that as a child our parents teach us manners? Help us to set boundaries and train us on even the simplest things like what is good and not good to eat? Sometimes we learn the importance of such lessons at the time of the teaching; and sometimes we don't realize the lesson until much later in life. As a youth you can eat just about anything and not gain an ounce. As you get older, however, an unhealthy eating habit can lead to a plethora of diseases not easily seen at the inception.

Likewise, while in school we learn reading, math, science, logic, and other subjects that at the time we complain we don't need. But as we grow up to be engineers, teachers, instructors, we learn that those subjects all have intrinsic value. Each precept learned stacks, precept upon precept, little by little (Isaiah 28:10). You should eat an elephant the same way you ought to approach life, one bite at a time.

Saul passed the first step and was found faithful to his father. Second, he was found faithful over the little he had. Saul was from the tribe of Benjamin and of all tribes to be born, he was from the smallest, the youngest, and the most humble (1 Samuel 9:20). In life we must remain humble and take our lessons with patience. The request Saul's father made of him, to go out and track down donkeys may not appear to be the mission of the century.

In fact, the mission could have been successful or ended in failure. Going on the search for the missing donkeys was a test of Saul's humility and a demonstration of his character.

Of all the animals to be recaptured, Saul's father had Saul look for the donkeys. 1 Samauel 9:3. What do donkeys represent? What was there function—purpose, or importance for Saul and his family? Donkeys are creatures that are reference several times in the Bible. The animal is able to bear very strong burdens and is considered a reliable helper to man.

This same animal is also a symbol of peace, industry, and wealth. Donkeys are the beast chosen by God to demonstrate humility, trust, and mark epic moments in people's lives. When Abraham used a donkey in Genesis 22:3 the concept of humility and trust was emphasized.

"Abraham got up early in the morning to saddle his donkey, a small act, yet one of obedience to the Lord in order to offer Isaac up to God."

It should be noted, Abraham didn't load up a horse to go and sacrifice his son, nor did he pack a bag that he carried on his own shoulders; but he saddled a donkey. A donkey represents a strong burden, a helper, and later in this account we find that the Lord gave the sacrifice and spared the life of Isaac. We learn that Abraham, was obedient to the Lord's command, and although his heart may have been heavy for the task given, he didn't waiver.

He trusted the Lord and obeyed His request and so found that the Lord was faithful. He provided the sacrifice and so much more. In Numbers 22:23-35 the Spirit of God fell on the second animal ever to speak to man, the donkey. He enabled the donkey to speak. The donkey did not open his mouth to curse man, to insult, or fight man. This animal is not a warring animal but a helper.

The donkey saw the angel of the Lord standing in the path with a sword drawn and he sought to help Balaam by disallowing him to cross. Balaam unaware of the animals desire to help him, beat the animal three times for disobeying his desire to press forward. After the third beating to this animal, the Lord gave the beast the ability to speak.

The donkey said to Balaam. "Am I not your own donkey, which you have always ridden, to this day? Have I been in the habit of doing this to you?" "No," he said.

The donkey asked a question to Balaam that highlighted the animal's faithfulness to him, his desire to help, and never let the man down. The beast was faithful and loyal with his life to the man; and yet this time the animal did not go in a direction to remain a helper to Balaam. When Balaam's eyes were opened and he saw the angel with the sword, he then knew he sinned. The donkey wasn't a stumbling block for the man but a helper. Had the donkey not spoke, had the donkey continued to walk, the angel said it would have slain Balaam because he was on a reckless path (Numbers 22:32-33).

Another account and perhaps one of the most profound, was that the Lord Jesus Christ also rode on a donkey. Why not a horse? A horse symbolizes war, vengeance, where as a donkey symbolizes peace, a helper, and one who bears a strong and heavy load for others. Jesus rode through the crowd on a donkey because He was sent to help us.

He was sent to restore peace and communion

between man and God. Jesus bore a load no other could bear so that man could be restored to the Father, the Creator of All. Jesus will be coming at the second coming riding on a horse. This horse does not represent peace, help, but war, judgment, vengeance, and vindication.

What else did we learn about the character of Saul? We learned he was committed to a task that demonstrated patience. Patience is a virtue and if you have ever prayed for patience you find that the Lord provides you with a test that works patience. Patience comes when you are in a state, or condition, where working out of your own strength nothing changes. Patience is learned when we realize our power is not able to move every mountain but the power of the Lord and in His timing working through man or other means.

We learn patience and are not given it. A

relationship that creates the foundation of patience is the relationship between parent and child. You don't know and understand patience until you parent or babysit children. Children require hearing instructions multiple times before they obey.

Children can be stiff-necked and hard to budge perhaps similar to a goat. A baby goat is formerly known as a kid and this is another adaption we have made to address children. Perhaps the reason for this connection is because children can be extremely stubborn. Try telling a one or two year old what they can or cannot do, and you find they have attitudes, attempt to throw temper tantrums, and even fight you!

But we are required to find corrective ways to address them and continue to teach the correct way to live. Through repetition and corrective behaviors they learn and we learn patience. The same way we learn to be patient with children is a similar example to how the Lord is also patient with us. God is the Father of His people, His children.

Have you noticed humility always produces patience, and patience builds character? The Lord says we ought to be like children (Matthew 18:3) so that we may enter into the Kingdom of God. That means we must be teachable; willing to listen and be obedient to Father God. The reason why we are commanded by God to obey our mother and father as children is because that same commandment as we get older we are to apply to God.

If you never learn to fear your mother and father, how can you know how to fear or reverence God? For that matter, how can we know to reverence officials, teachers, and elders? If we are not first taught to obey our mother and father we cannot be trained to obey and or respect anyone else.

Unruly children walk and run down a reckless path similar to Balaam and those who choose that path just may find an Angel swinging a sword before them and not the devil.

Thank the good Lord for the voices that are like the donkey in our lives that warn us to change direction and not to cross roads that could lead to death. There are many youths passing away and dropping like flies because they are living reckless lives and not heeding the direction of the Teacher.

The ultimate teacher is the Lord and we must take him seriously—respect Him because He is mighty and Holy. We aught not live recklessly because we never know when grace may run out. You don't want to look up and notice that the presence of God has left your life and you are walking alone. Remember, no matter where you go from here to stay humble and continue to listen to

God because children never outgrow their teacher (Luke 6:40).

Luke 6:40 says, "We are never above our teacher but are fully trained to be like our teacher." As believers we are to look like our Father. We are to look like Jesus without trying to replace His presence or Lordship in our life. Saul later stopped behaving like a child and attempts to be equal with God. He forgot this lesson and it cost him. To forget to reverence the Lord as Holy and wiser than ourselves, we fall into the trap of compromise.

When Saul did not follow orders from our Heavenly Father as he had learned to follow orders from his earthly father, He lost the presence of God. Saul didn't question his father on if it were wise to go out in search of the donkeys; he just did it because that was what he was told to do. Yet when the Lord told Him not to take or keep any man alive, he decided to disobey God because he thought he knew better.

Sometimes in life we are tempted to disobey an order from God and there are consequences for disobedience. An account that demonstrates the importance of obedience is the story of a prophet. This prophet was a mighty man of God. He believed in the Lord's power and ability to give the Hebrews the promised land. He had a personal relationship with God to where the Lord God gave him instructions and expected him to follow it (1 Kings 13:1-10).

This prophet was given a mission by God to deliver a message to a king. The Lord told him to deliver this message and not take anything from the king nor stay the night in the land. He was to go and hurry back home and not deviate from that plan.

This prophet did as he was requested. He went to the king, gave him a message, prayed with him for his hand to be restored, it was and the king offered him gifts, food, and lodging; which all he declined. He then set out to go home after his journey as the Lord commanded.

On his way home an old prophet came to him and told him he had a message from God for him. He told the prophet that the Lord told him he ought to eat and drink with him back at his house. The prophet decided to go back and eat and drink in the land the Lord told him not to.

He disobeyed the Lord's order. When the prophet left for home after what he thought was a good time that pleased the Lord, he found that his disobedience would cost him his life. The presence of God covered him when he was in His will. To deny a king was a grave insult, but the Lord's presence kept him safe and his objection to the king's offer was emphatic and not soft.

When he disobeyed the Lord's command and went back to eat and drink, the presence, the covering, the protection from the Lord was removed from His servant. A lion killed him when he returned to his journey home. The lion killed him and yet he was not devoured by it the Bible reads (1 Kings 13:26). The lion was not feasting on him because it was not hungry; but he was commissioned by God to end the journey and life of His servant because of disobedience.

What else did the prophet find next to the dead prophet's corpse? The old prophet told his sons to saddle his donkey as he departed for the body. When the prophet arrived at the body the lion and a donkey was standing nearby. The lion did not kill the donkey that looked onward at the prophet's dead flesh, nor did it eat the remains from him. It was on the back of the donkey on which the old prophet brought the body to town for a proper burial.

We must all learn to remember our humble begins. Never forget to remain like a child in the presence of God and take every Word from His mouth seriously. Your obedience or lack there of, could cost you your life. Even though Saul did not die instantly after his disobedience like the prophet, his relationship with God was dead and Saul was like the walking dead. He had no power and those close to him knew the anointing had left him. All the rage grew in him against the future king, David, because he was a constant reminder of his fall from grace.

You can operate in your gift, but also be dead inside, lacking the power, anointing, and presence of God. So, how did a man who started off on the right footing, get so far away from God? What went wrong you ask? Let's move to 1 Samuel 9:15-17 to see the light that's shed on this question.

KINGSHIP ANOINTING

The Grounds for the King

1 Samuel 9:15 – 17

15. Now the LORD had told Samuel in his ear a day before Saul came, saying,

16. Tomorrow about this time I will send thee a man out of the land of Benjamin, and thou shalt anoint him to be captain over my people Israel, that he may save my people out of the hand of the Philistines: for I have looked upon my people,

because their cry is come unto me.

17. And when Samuel saw Saul, the LORD said unto him, Behold the man whom I spake to thee of! This same shall reign over my people.

In life it is very tempting to attempt to speed up God's process for our life. In a society where microwaves are preferred over ovens, and are a requirement equal—if not greater than a stove. Patience is beyond a virtue for us but a challenge in our microwave society. No matter the actions we take, we cannot change the process that was set before the world began.

God set time in motion and for Him, time is not a factor nor a method to keep Him on schedule for He operates at will and by His will. Time is more beneficial to us as we are not omnipresent or omniscient so we need a way to track and keep up with each other. Time helps us to do that.

Can you imagine setting a meeting or making plans without a way to track the time? The answer should be no, because the chances of the meeting happening is slim if you both are not on the same page, operating by the same time, or have the same understanding.

Our number one goal should be to have our time align with God's timing, hence His will, His plans, and His vision for our lives. This might not sound great in the beginning because we all at one point in time thought we knew enough to determine what direction and tempo we want to march to in life; only to find that we were wrong and God had the right answer all a long. So, now that we understand and agree that this is true, we can proceed to the next step.

The next step requires us to get in step with God. We have to see the value in God's way, and choose His way over our own. We are to seek the Kingdom of God and all things will be added to us, not by seeking our desires and timing and expect God to catch up (Matthew 6:33).

Now, God's timing doesn't consult us for our opinion or approval. God speaks and what He says is final, perfect, truth, and must not be changed. The Lord requires our obedience to His command, because in the Bible it reads, "You are not a true believer unless you follow His commandments (John 14:15)." In addition He says, obedience is better than sacrifice and His sheep knows His voice (John 10:27).

The Lord gives us all gifts because we are His children and He prepares us to serve His kingdom. Spiritual gifts are a much talked about subject among believers and churchgoers because until you know your gifts you cannot be certain of your purpose. Your purpose and gifts are locked into each other and they both work hand in hand.

Although there are test, gismos, websites, articles and books on how to determine your gift(s), the final approval for your gift(s) must come from the Lord. The test you can take, people you can speak to, and other ways people go about finding their gifts is not a bad idea or way of discovery, but never leave God out of the process. When we leave God out of this vital part of our walk as a believer, we run the risk of being misplaced in the body and function more as a plague or cancerous cell— foreign, than function as a vital part to the body of Christ. There are two passages in particular that talks about spiritual gifts and define such gifting's.

First, in 1 Corinthians 12 we learn that gifts

from the Lord includes wisdom, knowledge, faith, healing, miracles, prophecy, distinguishing between spirits (discernment), tongues, and the interpretation of tongues (1 Corinthians 12:7-10). All these are empowered by one and the same Spirit, God, who apportions to each individually as He wills (1 Corinthians 12:11). The Lord has a plan for your life and your gift is an asset for how He intends to get you there.

In Ephesians 4:11 we learn of the spiritual gifts that make up what is commonly referred to as the five-fold ministry. The five-fold ministry is made up of apostles, prophets, evangelist, preachers, and teachers. These gifts are bestowed upon God's children for the edification of the body of Christ. Gifts are not given for man to decide how to use them but for the Lord to instruct their use.

Let's revisit the parable that paints the best

picture of spiritual gifts briefly (Matthew 25:14-30). God gave three people gifts, which was reflected

in talents or shekels. The three varied in what they did with the talents, but the two that did the will of the Lord and returned a harvest, used their talent for the edification of the Kingdom got a greater reward. The foolish man, who buried the talent and returned nothing on top of what was given, was called wicked and casted out the gates.

Choose to use your talent for God and don't bury the gifts God has given you but trust Him to give you instruction. In the case of Saul, instruction was very much needed as he didn't appear to be qualified to be the King of the Hebrew nation; in fact no man is qualified but God to lead. In order for him to have a fighting chance to lead them he had to seek the Lord every step of the way, as there was no king prior to him. There was something about Saul that the Lord liked that made Him choose Saul to become king.

One of Saul's gifts included leadership, and two other gifts attributed to him were wisdom and knowledge. These gifts were birthed in him long before he realized. The first lesson any good leader aught to learn or possess is a teachable spirit. Before you can lead you must first know how to follow. Saul had to hear the voice of the Lord and follow the commands of God, because he had to lay the foundation.

Saul proved in his youth he was capable and raised to listen to the voice of his father; likewise, he had to be able to listen to his heavenly Father's Voice. If we don't pass the first step we can't make it to the next. Saul's next step was to learn the road and after learning the road he could then lead others. He had to spend lots of time with God and God's appointed people to develop and mature the talents God saw in him at his youth. By developing your gifts, it allows for the Lord to call you into the game.

When in sports camp, training, or perhaps even in band camp, you have to learn routines and are required to be active in practice. If you are not active in practice the coach will not see what you can do, so he will not put you in the game. Practice must be taking just as serious as the real game.

When you study the Word, do it with purpose because lives depend on it. Once your training is complete it is time to take you out of the simulation and put you in the game. Once Saul finished his training it was time to put him in the game. The donkey mission was practice; the game is being king over the Hebrew nation.

In verse 15, we also see another gift at work,

prophecy. Samuel was called as a young man to serve the Lord, but before he became the prophet we know in the Bible, he first swept floors, did dishes, and learned the church. Even when God first called his name, and he answered, he was not ready to be put in the game because he wasn't mature in his gift. But when his time came, he served the Lord God and provided accounts for you and I.

So you see, committing to your gifting is ultra important. When we follow God, we must remember it is never about us, but always about God and His kingdom. Samuel and Saul were stewards for the owner; the owner is the Lord God Almighty. We are all required to function in the body as His Spirit works over all and works through all and in all (Ephesians 4:4)

Notice, it was not Saul telling God to use him but it was God that saw Him and chose Him. God chooses us, and if we want Him to draw near to us, we must first draw near to Him; and we do that by first acknowledging Him and purifying our hearts (James 4:8). A note worthy point to also consider, when God gives us gifts He anoints our gifts.

Saul had no possible way of growing to be king in the natural. He was from the lowest tribe, that was also the smallest, and if there were a campaign or vote that would have taken place like in the current day, he had no wealth to run his campaign. With the King's anointing over his life, however, the Lord gave him a position he could have never earned. Yes, He does the same thing with you and I. The presence of the Lord, the anointing married to our gift(s) will open doors no man or demonic force can shut.

Victory Through the Presence of God

1 Samuel 14: 47 – 48

47. So Saul took the kingdom over Israel, and fought against all his enemies on every side, against Moab, and against the children of Ammon, and against Edom, and against the kings of Zobah, and against the Philistines: and whithersoever he turned himself, he vexed them.

48. And he gathered a host, and smote the Amalekites, and delivered Israel out of the hands of them that spoiled them.

I made a bold statement about how the doors the Lord opens for you that no one can shut. Allow me to justify that truth with Deuteronomy 28:3-11. The Lord says, "We are blessed in the city and blessed in the field;" furthermore He says, He will make us to "prosper" and "abound" in everything we do. This same truth is supported by 1 Samuel 14:47-48 when the Bible states when you carry the Presence of God, any divine assignment that you carry out, the final result is victory.

When we walk with the Spirit of God it is equivalent and should pack as much power as walking with the Ark of the Covenant. Keep in mind the heart and holiness you must maintain to be near the ark. The presence of God has to be with you at all times for the victory to be yours and for Him to fight your battle. When the Lord fights your battle it may not make sense, it may not look good to the natural eye, but the spiritual eye sees all and you will win.

Saul was able to defeat the Moabites, Ammonites, Edomites, and etc. not because he was the King of Israel but because the Presence of God was over His life. Later in his life, if he was not already convinced the power was not his own but of God because when the presence of the Lord left him, his glory went as well. The same blessings He gave in Deuteronomy 28 were followed by curses for those that didn't do what the Lord said.

Being a child of God requires that we maintain the Presence of God in our lives. We must never waiver or stop having faith or trusting in Him. We don't have to be strong warriors or the best at anything for the Lord to bless us. He says to us, in our weakness He is made strong, so take courage if you don't feel you are the best or you lack resources to excel; that will not stop the plans God has for you (2 Corinthians 12:9-10)!

Don't let adversity shake your belief that the Presence of God is not in your life. You see, it is during the battles that the Lord can be glorified because He makes us triumphant over our problems, situations, and our enemies. Challenges will come to us all. Saul had battle after battle that he had to fight, and God gave him the victory.

That same God is able to give you victory also in any facet of your life and surely where He commanded you to go He is able to pave the way. Keep the Presence of God in your life and conform your lifestyle to a victorious one. Where the Spirit of the Lord is, our battles will always be won and the favor of the Lord will be on our lives.

THE PROPHETIC ANOINTING GOES WITH OBEDIENCE

The Command for Ruling

1 Samuel 10:7

7. And let it be, when these signs are come unto thee, that thou do as occasion serve thee; for God is with thee.

If you have been gifted with a gift from the Lord there are requirements and responsibilities assigned to you to operate in your gift according to Godly standards. In the case of Saul, the first anointing that God used Prophet Samuel to give over Saul's life, was a Kingship anointing; there is evidence also that Saul had a prophetic anointing as well (1 Samuel 10-6-7, 10-13). Saul was able to communicate with God directly and this had to be a requirement, as another man never had this post. God personalized his quest for Saul and spoke with him directly. He was active in governing over Israel and gave Saul access to His divine throne room by way of the prophetic.

This gift was not and even into the future bestowed on every king. Many men were king in the Bible and they all did not have access to the throne room of God. I believe God gifted Saul with the ability of having access to Him so that He could stay encouraged and not faint or doubt. When you hear the Voice of the Lord, you have peace and there is nothing you fear.

Saul coming from an inferior background, stepping up in a major way to lead warriors in battle, and take a throne without any experience was a large undertaking. With the Presence of God and the Voice of God in his ear, He had to feel confident in God's ability to deliver Israel no matter the circumstance. In addition, God gifted him with the prophetic so that the manifestation of total obedience would continuously come forth throughout his reign. "For I know My sheep, My sheep know Me and they hear My voice (John 10:27).

The Divine Command

1 Samuel 15: 3

3. Now go and smite Amalek, and utterly destroy all that they have, and spare them not; but slay both man and woman, infant and suckling, ox and

sheep, camel and ass.

Saul was very acquainted with the Presence of God and seeing the manifestation with signs and wonders. His prophetic gifting appeared in less than 24 hours after Samuel prophesied it. He was seen doing miracle after miracle including his ability to speak in the prophetic. Saul was following the Voice of the Lord and reaping the benefits from his obedience and trust in God's Word to him.

Your obedience to God guarantees the stability of the Presence of God in your life. Saul learned this, mastered this, but did he keep it at heart?

In our lives it is possible for us to reach a low point. We can experience a life-altering situation where we are the victim, and by God's grace He delivers us and we become the victor. When you have victory after victory, some may loose sight on why they are victorious. When we displace God, and attempt to rob Him of His glory, we are out of His will. When we are out of His will we can forfeit our blessings.

Have you ever felt the frustration of encountering ungrateful children? Children who since they were born, they were cared for, provided for, feed by, and loved on by their parents. When the child grew up, they went to college, graduated, then got a great job in part because of their parents. Then all of a sudden they are too busy for their parents. They no longer care for the quality of life for their parents.

The prodigal son is the prime example for how some children who are raised well, encounter what appears to be a blessing, money, and when they get it they loose there mind. Something happens to man when we encounter wealth, riches, power that if we have not girded our flesh and weighed it down with the Word, our flesh will attempt to over throw the Spirit. Sometimes this is a subtle change in thinking, actions, or belief that leads to a world of regret and sin.

In 1 Samuel 15:3 The Lord told him to go (command) and attack the Amalekites. Kill the king, kill all the people, and destroy everything that they had. When the Lord gives a command it is imperative you, we listen, because sometimes there are no redo's.

The prophet didn't get a redo; he was mauled by the lion and died for disobedience (1 Samuel 17:36). Ananias and Sapphira were struck dead from not giving to the church what they committed—no redo (Acts 5:1-11). Achan in Joshua was told to take nothing but he took coins, a coat for his wife, and this cost him his life and the lives of his entire family—no redo (Joshua 7:21).

In your Christian walk with Christ, do you always remain sensitive to the voice of God? We must in the situation of a divine command or we run the risk of removing the presence and protection of God from our lives.

He Was Disobedient

1 Samuel 15:7 – 9

7. And Saul smote the Amalekites from Havilah until thou comest to Shur, that is over against Egypt.

8. And he took Agag the king of the Amalekites alive, and utterly destroyed all the people with the edge of the sword.

9. But Saul and the people spared Agag, and the best of the sheep, and of the oxen, and of the fatlings, and the lambs, and all that was good, and would not utterly destroy them: but everything that was vile and refuse, that they destroyed utterly.

Saul did what was tempting to any man to do; to consider and try to rationalize the Word God gave to benefit his liking—don't do this. Don't try to bend the Truth to fit your lifestyle, your desire, your ministry platform, or anything else. Bending the truth even a little makes it a lie and the Truth is not in it.

The Bible instructs us not to add nor take away from the Word (Revelation 22:18-20). When we change and alter God's Word to fit our own liking we have accepted another gospel and it is as Paul ask "Who has bewitched you (Galatians 3:1)?" Saul was jumped or succumbed to the spirit of iniquity. Iniquity is a premeditated choice and continuance of sin without repentance.

The Lord specifically told him to destroy everything that the Amalekites had in their possession and not leave a thing of theirs. King Saul, however, only destroyed some of their things, killed most of the people, took the glamorous and glittering things, healthy animals, and spared the life of their King. Now, what was going on in the mind of Saul that seduced him to believe—that "A," God would be okay with him changing His plans?

"B," that there would be no consequence for his disobedience—or that he could bare the punishment? The trick of the enemy is to have your eyes set on one thing, while he is plotting to have his overall goal accomplished, which is to have you fall. King Saul was tricked much like Eve was trick in the garden to believe disobedience to God's Word would be okay because of good intentions. Sometimes, aren't we capable of thinking the end justifies the means?

This is not an uncommon situation and many of us—all of us, because we are all tempted to disobey God, if we sin we distance ourselves from God and we embrace a lie over truth. In hindsight, we have all made decision that we grew to regret. Thank the Lord for his mercy and goodness because He allows us to repent and turn back. But for some they are not able to turn back and are given over to a reprobate mind until God allows them to come to themself (Romans 1:28).

Nebuchadnezzar was a man who doubted God, and He allowed him—the king to loose his mind, until the Lord permitted him to come to himself (Daniel 4:32-33). There is the two million dollar question I can think to ask Saul:

- What went wrong?
- Who or what made you decide to disobey God?

These questions can best be answered by what is in the scriptures. The scriptures provide the key evidences that document the compromise. When we allow for mans voice to be louder than God, we run the risk of loosing site of God. The Bible says that the world is in war with God, the WORD, aka Jesus.

How did Saul, who was blessed with so much, a kingship, the prophetic, salvation, and communion with God, forsake God, the Creator of the Universe, for so little? Traditions of men, acceptance, appreciation, approbation, he would find soon will dissipate as another comes up in his place not a moment too soon. The devil pursues you until he has you, then he disappears but watches you drown while he roars into laughter.

THE EVIDENCE OF COMPROMISE

Materialistic

1 Samuel 15:13-15

13. And Samuel came to Saul: and Saul said unto him, Blessed be thou of the LORD: I have performed the commandment of the LORD.

14. And Samuel said, What meaneth then this bleating of the sheep in mine ears, and the lowing of the oxen which I hear?

15. And Saul said, They have brought them from the Amalekites: for the people spared the best

of the sheep and of the oxen, to sacrifice unto the LORD thy God; and the rest we have utterly destroyed.

Saul forgot that Samuel was a man of God and could hear the Voice of the Lord. He must have, because how could he come before a prophet of the Most High God and think he could conceal the truth from God? He believed in a very nasty dream, a lie, and when you accept a lie as truth, you have to support the lie with more lies.

Saul did not follow the command of the Lord but rested in his own thinking, understanding, and deviated from the command. The Bible tells us not to lean on our own understand but rely on every Word from God (Proverbs 3:5-6). Saul is without any excuse because he could hear the Voice of the Lord directly. He had the presence of God operating in his life to an undeniable degree and yet he thought he could lie and hide like Adam and Eve when they sinned.

We will not be able to sweet talk God or conceal our true heart's desire, intent, nor defend our actions with lies. God is omnipresent, omnipotent, and knows all and He especially knows the hearts and desires of His children (Jeremiah 1:5). "Before I formed you in the womb I knew you, before you were born I set you apart; I appointed you as a prophet to the nations." God had a plan for Saul, and He worked that plan, He perfects every work He starts (Philippians 1:6). It's a shame, God finished a work and Saul unravelled as much of it as he could with his compromise.

You can see clearly that anytime one goes wrong, or disobeys God's command, it can be very difficult for that person to come back. Unlike what David did when he realized he messed up, he repented, Saul decided to hide or avoid that truth. The reason it could be so hard to come back to God, is because from the bottom of Saul's heart when he sinned against God he knew the presence of God was over his life. All sins can be forgiving except blaspheming against the Holy Spirit (Mark 3:28-30).

Saul was supposed to go and report to Samuel and yet Samuel didn't hear from Saul but had to go and confront Saul. How many of us after we have fallen, we were M.I.A (missing in action). Nobody can call you on the phone or won't see you in church. You have been shifted away, separated from God and you maybe totally content with that separation because to confront God would mean exposing the truth; you disobeyed God.

When Samuel confronted Saul, he made it as if everything was fine. When Samuel made bare the things that were thought to be secret, Saul didn't confess but lied and said it was for God. How can we sin against God then say we sinned for God? Fresh and salt water cannot come out of the same vessel neither can disobedience be supported by the notion "I sinned to please God;" it is an oxymoron (James 3:11).

I believe the prophet Samuel was there, not only to rebuke King Saul for his disobedience to the Lord but also to extend an opportunity for him to get in right step with God. Saul was given a chance to admit, fess up, and repent for his action but instead he blamed others. When the Lord was walking in the garden in the cool of the day, He approached Adam and Eve for there transgressions who also blamed each other and the serpent (Genesis 3:8-13).

This did not stop God's judgment, for one they lied to God to His face, then tried to explain why lying was okay. Not a good idea. Saul didn't realize at the time, it was a privilege to acknowledge his sin and repent. God desired to forgive Him because sin causes a separation between God and us (Isaiah 59:2-3).

Christians and non-believers can fall into this trap, whereby we blame others about our situation. Stop blaming people and acknowledge any shortcoming of obedience in your life, for God is still there for you. Keep your allegiance to God.

Change Allegiance From God to Another

1 Samuel 15:17 – 19

17. And Samuel said, When thou wast little in thine own sight, wast thou not made the head of the tribes of Israel, and the LORD anointed thee king over Israel?

18. And the LORD sent thee on a journey, and said, Go and utterly destroy the sinners the Amalekites, and fight against them until they be consumed.

19. Wherefore then didst thou not obey the voice of the LORD, but didst fly upon the spoil, and didst evil in the sight of the LORD?

When King Saul did not own his sin and repent, his allegiance shifted from doing the work of the Lord to doing and justifying his own plans. He was no longer concerned for how his sin hurt God nor concerned about how his sin affected him. He got away from his first love and began the transition of allegiance from God to satan. Serving your self is lukewarm and alone we are no match for the enemy. He refused to repent but chose instead to continue blaming others for his choices during the invasion; he could have changed their actions as Joshua corrected violations in the past.

He was the leader over the tribes of Israel; the Lord anointed him as the King of Israel and gave him orders. Therefore, those people he was blaming, he was responsible for and mandated by God to govern. Saul was king and his people took orders from him, so by extension he made the order to let it stand. If this was not Saul's idea in the inception, it became his choice and he sided with the voice of men over the command of God. In this dispensation of the Christian journey, who are you accountable to--is it to God or to man?

While you're thinking, ways to determine where your allegiance lies, consider how you make decisions. Do you align truth with the Bible or society? Do you take the Bible as is or do you filter the Word through your ideas and society norms? Do you allow the Word to permeate your thoughts? If your thoughts come before the Word or you consider societal norms to be appropriate over scripture, your allegiance is not with God. Follow the Bible, or you will be judged by it!

Don't allow the opinion of man to be your first allegiance. We are not called to question God's authority; we are allowed however, to ask Him questions. God gives us permission to come boldly to the throne of grace (Hebrew 4:16). We serve a mighty and powerful God who is the King of all Kings and He sets all men that are in high places. Nothing in life happens without his knowledge (Lamentations 3:37).

Justification and Denial

1 Samuel 15: 20 – 22

20. Then Saul said to Samuel, "I did obey the voice

of the LORD, and went on the mission on which the LORD sent me, and have brought back Agag the king of Amalek, and have utterly destroyed the Amalekites.

21. "But the people took some of the spoil, sheep and oxen, the choicest of the things devoted to destruction, to sacrifice to the LORD your God a Gilgal."

22. And Samuel said, Hath the Lord as great delight in burnt offerings and sacrifices, as in obeying the voice of the Lord? Behold, to obey is better than sacrifice, and to hearken than the fat of rams."

To read that King Saul abdicate he was doing a work to benefit the Lord when he knew he was lying made matters worst for him. Even Samuel pleaded with him "why lie?" An old saying attributed to grandmothers, mothers, and big mommas around the world, "Tell the truth and shame the devil" was the piece of advice King Saul needed to initiate.

When we parent our children, we are not as upset with them that they messed up, but when they lie about it; that is where discipline becomes mandatory. We must learn not to hide our sin from God, because it is not possible to keep a secret from Him anyhow. He sees all and knows all; so we are only running and lying to ourselves. God knows the truth because He is the Truth.

Not only was Saul lying, but he was also attempting to justify his wrong to Samuel. We have clearly lost our way when God sends people into our lives to rebuke us and we try to convert them to be on our side; which is on the wrong side. We must not buck at rebuke, but embrace correction and pray for each other because the prayers of the righteous avails much (James 5:16). Saul was in front of Samuel and said your God as if there God was no longer the same.

Saul turned away and continued to lie and attempt to justify himself. He wanted Samuel and most importantly God to accept and condone his actions. He was trying to tell God to accept wrong as right and right as wrong. This is why Prophet Samuel was open to tell him that obedience (doing the will of God) is better than sacrifice (works). In other words "What you say you are, is not important than what you do."

We all have to remember, and believe in this Christian journey we must not justify our sins before God or his leaders when rebuked. Justifying our sins will destroy anyone who operates with this false thinking. God is here and able to forgive you if you only ask. There is nothing that will set you too far away from God, outside of blaspheming against the Holy Spirit.

So do not run from the saving grace that we all so desperately need. It doesn't matter how many times we fall down but how many times we stand. The Bible says we ought to forgive 77 times and surely God is more merciful than any man (Matthew 18:21-22). Remain open and naked before God and confess your sins; He is faithful and just to forgive you from all unrighteousness.

WHEN SIN IS ACKNOWLEDGED

Admission of Error

1 Samuel 15:24-26

24. "Yes, I have sinned," Saul replied. "I disobeyed the Lord's command and your instructions. I was afraid of my men and did what they wanted.

25. But now I beg you, forgive my sin and go back with me, so that I can worship the Lord."

26. "I will not go with you," Samuel answered. "You rejected the Lord's command, and He rejected you as King of Israel."

There are always seasons and timings in our lives when God gives us the opportunity to repent and accept the grace that's bestowed on all Christian. If you don't discern God's timing or take grace for granted, you will miss the mark. King Saul is exhibit "A" for what happens when you miss the mark and close the door on grace. Because King Saul did not accept grace when it was given he welcomed judgment upon his life.

Have you ever seen the people that are in dire straits lacking food, clothes, health, unable to physically get stuff accomplished reject the help that is sent? The Lord sends along a person with a heart and the ability to help them and they reject them. Instead of the person who is in need receiving the help, they turn it down and send the person away. When we do that we are left to our own demise and will continue to struggle to get the job done.

It is not wise to turn away the hand of God no matter what any man or devil might say to change your mind. The Bible says, "…for those who stand with me now, I will stand with you later (Matthew 10:32)." We do not want to be disowned by Jesus or God the Father because we have rejected Him. It is a huge insult for us to reject the Lord God knowing He died for us when we were still sinners that hated Him (Romans 5:10). In Luke 9:26 the Bible also says, "Whoever is ashamed of me and my words, the Son of Man will be ashamed of them when He comes in His glory and in the glory of the Father and of the holy angels."

Do you remember when you were a kid and you strategized on the friends and people you should keep close to you? In life there is no difference. We naturally seek out people that we can't allow and or do not desire to be a foe but a friend.

God is one that you do not want to be a foe but has to be a friend; no one can box with God and win. When we become a friend of God it is personal when we reject Him. Is there a man, woman, person, place, or thing that can separate us from the Love of God (Romans 8:31-39)?

This separation between God and us is usually kindled by fear of rejection by our peers, or other men and women who don't value our God or His Word. When we allow these voices and opinions to be greater than God's, we are embarrassed and pride creeps up that prohibits us from owning up. In this particular verse King Saul acknowledged the fact that he had sinned and disobeyed God's command only after much prying by Samuel. Why wasn't he able to voice out his sin? He admitted to being more afraid of people and their opinions than fearing God.

His allegiance became to man instead of God. You see Saul did not realize the people were attracted to the light that was in him not him. People saw Saul as a victor and so did the devil.

The devil loves nothing more than to see you and I fall from the place that God has appointed us. Saul did not realize, by siding with man, siding with the devil, he lost the presence of God. Once he looses the Presence of God, he would loose the approbation from the people.

We must maintain the Christian dispensation of obedience to the Lord's voice no matter what king, queen, friend, or foe has to say. When we maintain the Presence of God over our life we don't and are not supposed to compromise nor listen to the voice of other people. King Saul's biggest mistake was listening to the voices of men instead of obeying the voice of God. Saul fell from grace and shattered his purpose. According to this passage, God determined he was no longer fit to serve His purpose and He released him from being the King of Israel.

While reflecting on Saul's biggest mistake let's explore what happens when the Spirit of the Lord leaves. What condition do you perceive Saul to be in? Should he still be confident? The Bible says that God is our strength and my shield (Psalm 28:7)! If He leaves, is the inverse true? Saul is now weak and open to attack, but guess what, in our weakness to the Lord, God remains our strength (2 Corinthians 12:9); but what about those that have not the Lord? What happens in this weaken state?

SPIRIT OF CARNALITY

Challenges

1 Samuel 17:23-24

23. And as he talked with them, behold, there came up the champion, the Philistine of Gath, Goliath by name, out of the armies of the Philistines, and spake according to the same words: and David heard them.

24. And all the men of Israel, when they saw the man, fled from him, and were sore afraid.

When the spirit of the Lord leaves your life,

grace and mercy goes with it. Saul was now left weak and humble as he was before the presence of the Lord dwelled with him. Now, he is just that simple boy that is grown according to years but without the help of the Lord his strength had left him. When we loose our position and favor in the eyes of the Lord, two specific spirits linked to carnality raise their head. The first is envy and the second is jealousy.

When David came on the scene to fight Goliath he exposed the weakness in Saul to the nation. Why was the king, who led many battles before and won, now fearful like the other people to fight Goliath? Where was his confidence, strength, and leadership? The confidence was in the presence of the Lord.

Now that the voice of God was not in his ear o lead, Saul was on his own. He sought out other men that could help him take care of his problems.

Saul lost his ability to lean on God because he chose to lean on man. He is now left to struggle to accomplish the task and challenges ahead of him.

Angry About Other People's Success

1 Samuel 18:8

8. And Saul was very wroth, and the saying displeased him; and he said, They have ascribed unto David ten thousands, and to me they have ascribed but thousands: and what can he have more but the kingdom?

When the young man, David, defeated Goliath his renown increased among the people. Of course, prior to King David having the courage to face the giant, he too was anointed with a kingly anointing by Samuel. He was also the youngest, smallest, the most humble as his chances of inquiring any wealth was slim.

He had several older brothers entitled to his father's inheritance long before he would receive a thing. The Lord took this humble soul, same as he took Saul, and began to lift him up. He had to fight lions and bears before he fought Goliath so he too had test to prepare him for his journey.

Saul knew all too well what was happening with young David better than anyone. When he saw David he was reminded of his past, of his humble beginning. He started to hear of the fame of David and the people's voice placed David above his position. The words of the Almighty God through his servant Samuel were becoming real to him. Saul became envious of the song the people sang lifting David above his fame.

The people said David killed ten thousand and

Saul only thousands. The people that Saul allowed to make him fall from grace are now the people that have turned their backs on him. The fame he grew all too comfortable with having had disappeared and his envy was kindled against David.

The Spirit of Jealousy

1 Samuel 18:9

9. And Saul eyed David from that day and forward. But the spirit of envy festered in Saul and jealousy was a close twin to his new envy.

Saul, once the great leader, the favored by God, is now an outcaste looking on another to obtain and fulfill the purpose that was once on his life. There is nothing that makes a person envious and jealous than seeing another excel in their footsteps. When we choose not to walk in our gifts or obey the voice of the Lord, God will find another that is willing and able (Isaiah 6:8).

Don't allow envy and jealousy to take root, because it will cause you to miss out on your destiny. It is possible for us to get off track in life but there is redemption and the Lord is a redeemer of time (Psalm 103:4). We should not envy each other's gifts, as we all have gifts to function in the body of Christ.

If you see another prospering beyond you, keep them in prayer, and learn what you can from their testimony. No one elevates in God without learning some tough lessons. Keep your faith and eyes stayed on Jesus so that you may not fall into the trap of carnality. Carnality is not only brought on by the desire to appease other people but also to appease your own desire.

EVIDENCE GOD'S PRESENCE HAS DEPARTED

Human Thinking

1 Samuel 16:17-19

17. Saul ordered them, "Find me a man who plays well and bring him to me".

18. One of his attendants said, "Jesse, of the town of Bethlehem, has a son who is a good musician. He is also a brave and handsome man, good soldier and an able speaker. The Lord is with him.

19. So Saul sent messengers to Jesse to say, "Send me your son David the one who takes care of your sheep."

Experience

When the joy of the Lord is not our strength the works of the flesh takes pre-eminence over your life. When Saul was seeking a replacement to sustain his joy, he sought out a remedy. Although music didn't solve his problems, it did sooth his emotions—fear. He was frustrated to find that the same one he hated was the one to save him from himself.

Funny, how we try to make God our problem, only to find that He is the solution. The best harp player in the country was the same one gaining more victories and ordained to take his place as king, David. When we attempt to find solutions to filling he vacancy of loosing the Presence of God in our lives, we learn that there is no replacement. Natural and narcotic highs are fleeting and at the end, when the music stops and the high fades, the same anxieties are still there.

When David arrived to play for King Saul his likeable spirit and the Presence of the Lord could be seen all over him; even Saul's children could see it. It's amazing how everyone has a hunger to be in the light even if they do not live according to the light. You never hear about someone looking for a selfish, self-centered, unfriendly, unkind, unloving person; but the exact opposite! Saul's son, Jonathan, meet David and the two became good friends.

The Lord stayed near to Saul enough for him to keep his eye on the Lord and know that God was moving; God is just no longer moving with him. God had moved his anointing to David and like in Psalms, He made all love him including Saul's son. When the

Lord wants to show you something, there is no limit to what He will do to bring you in remembrance of Him. No matter what we do to try and escape God, there is nothing created that can fill the hole God leaves behind when He exits your life but more of Him.

The Spirit of Fear

1 Samuel 17:8-10

8. And he stood and cried unto the armies of Israel, and said unto them, Why are ye come out to set your battle in array? Am not I a Philistine, and ye servants to Saul? choose you a man for you, and let him come down to me.

9. If he be able to fight with me, and to kill me, then will we be your servants: but if I prevail

against him, and kill him, then shall ye be our servants, and serve us.

10. And the Philistine said, I defy the armies of Israel this day; give me a man, that we may fight together.

Another shift that takes place in our lives when the Presence of God departs, we're no longer confident, and fear takes its rightful place, replacing our trust in God with fear. Have you ever notice when people are fearful they will give away everything to be secure? Even if the security is a false security, because nothing created by man lasts forever. When you hand everything over for security you find that you loose everything. No man can ever promise you security because we are neither omnipresent nor sovereign.

Only the Lord is sovereign over all the earth and

can save, protect, and keep you no matter the circumstance. There is a large space in all of our lives that can only be filled with God's Presence, also known as His Spirit. If that place is empty, the devil and demons take up residence and alone you cannot cast them out. The help of the Lord keeps the demons away, resist the devil and he will flee (James 4:7). Well, if you have not submitted yourself to God, by what authority can you send the demons fleeing?

When the twelve disciples were working and carrying out ministry, they came across a strange spirit, a demon that told them, "Paul and Jesus I know, but who are you (Acts 19:15)?" You see your spirit bares witness to who and what you are. If you have the Spirit of the Lord your actions will bear fruit to validate your claims (Matthew 7:16). Saul's fear was exposed in this passage and another valid point is also revealed. Saul no longer had trust in the Lord to deliver his enemies to him and grant him victory.

Saul was scared, fearful and rightfully so, that he would die if he battled anyone. So he had to continue the journey he started and rely on people to attempt to save him. Saul must have had many sleepless nights and this is obvious because most of the time he was worried on if David would attack and take the throne by force. With the songs the people sang, he wasn't even sure if the kingdom would side with him or David should he invade. So, he had to sleep with one eye open.

When Trust Fades in God

1 Samuel 17:33

33. And Saul said to David, Thou art not able to go against this Philistine to fight with him: for thou art but a youth, and he a man of war from his youth.

In this passage Saul lost all faith in God and trust

only in the might of men. He believed the Philistine would devour David because he was focused and looking on the flesh instead of peering into the spiritual. The spiritual realm he could not peer into, because the Presence and the Spirit of the Lord had left him. Without the Spirit of God we cannot see the world as it truly is but as it looks to the naked eye.

This is living life without faith so you can only walk by sight. When David talked about fighting Goliath, Saul thought he was out of his mind. The Bible says, "God uses the foolish things in order to shame those that think they are wise (1Corinthians 1:27)." So yes, God is able to use a willing vessel that doesn't stand tall, has nothing but a rock, slingshot, and Faith. Faith in God makes you mighty and able to tear down any stronghold.

Saul forgot about the battles he won that were not won because of strategy and ideas from him but because of the Presence of God. It is very easy to take your health for granted, people for granted, and even God for granted. When your body is up and working as it should many of us hardly think about the food we eat. If we exercise on a regular basis or get enough sleep. The moment that body starts to breakdown and sickness creeps upon us, we then look to receive healing and perhaps seek out change.

If we are not careful we can misuse God's Presence and be so comfortable with knowing He is there that we forget to acknowledge His Presence. The Lord God is holy and we must acknowledge Him like a Holy King and not even remotely similar to a man. If we treat the Lord like we treat our bodies, or like we treat people, we can take Him for granted and not realize when He left our lives.

Saul thought his strength was in himself, his title, his kingdom, the things the Lord made him a steward over and not an owner of. We are all simply stewards because we can't take it with us. Don't sell your soul short; the kingdom is awaiting those that seek His Kingdom first (Matthew 6:33).

"But seek ye first the kingdom of God, and his righteousness; and all these things shall be added unto you."

Unanswered Prayer

1 Samuel 28:6

6. And when Saul inquired of The LORD, the LORD answered him not, neither by dreams, nor by Urim, nor by prophets.

Saul's woes kept increasing as a result of his disobedience to the Lord, when you carefully analyze this very scripture, it shows how his prayer was unanswered, another sign of the departed Presence of God is when your prayers are no more heard neither answered.

Seeking Mediums to To replace God

1 Samuel 28: 7-18

7. Then said Saul unto his servants, Seek me a woman that hath a familiar spirit, that I may go to her, and inquire of her. And his servants said to him, Behold, there is a woman that hath a familiar spirit at Endor.

8. And Saul disguised himself, and put on other raiment, and he went, and two men with him, and they came to the woman by night: and he said, I pray thee, divine unto me by the familiar spirit, and bring me him up, whom I shall name unto thee.

9. And the woman said unto him, Behold, thou knowest what Saul hath done, how he hath cut off those that have familiar spirits, and the wizards, out of the land: wherefore then layest thou a snare for my life, to cause me to die? 10 And Saul swore to her by the LORD, saying, As the LORD liveth, there shall no punishment happen to thee for this thing.

11. Then said the woman, Whom shall I bring up unto thee? And he said, Bring me up Samuel

12. And when the woman saw Samuel, she cried with a loud voice: and the woman spoke to Saul, saying, Why hast thou deceived me? For thou art Saul.

13. And the king said unto her, Be not afraid: for what sawest thou? And the woman said unto Saul, I saw gods ascending out of the earth.

14. And he said unto her, What form is he of? And she said, An old man cometh up; and he is covered with a mantle. And Saul perceived that it was Samuel, and he stooped with his face to the ground, and bowed himself.

15. And Samuel said to Saul, Why hast thou disquieted me, to bring me up? And Saul answered, I am sore distressed; for the Philistines make war against me, and God is departed from me, and answereth me no more, neither by prophets, nor by dreams: therefore I have called thee, that thou mayest make known unto me what I shall do.

16. Then said Samuel, Wherefore then dost thou ask of me, seeing the LORD is departed from thee, and is become thine enemy? 17 And the LORD hath done to him, as he spake by me: for the LORD hath rent the kingdom out of thine hand, and given it to thy neighbor, even to David:

18. Because thou obeyedst not the voice of the LORD, nor executedst his fierce wrath upon Amalek, therefore hath the LORD done this thing unto thee this day.

19. Moreover the LORD will also deliver Israel with thee into the hand of the Philistines: and to morrow shalt thou and thy sons be with me: the LORD also shall deliver the host of Israel into the hand of the Philistines.

Another shift that takes place in our lives when the Presence of God departs, we start to seek other mediums of powers, Saul started looking for another solution to his woes and neglecting the Lord that made him a king, these are serious lessons that needs to be noted especially when you no longer hear from God as a result of the departed Presence of God.

THE CONCLUSION

I trust you were blessed from reading "The Big Mistake of Saul." You took a journey to obtain strategic knowledge through understanding the repercussions for the decisions Saul made. His decisions were both positive and negative. I believe that you see the value in his obedience and learned lessons from the mistakes Saul made. Perhaps, during your lifetime you experienced a similar aftermath. This book is not intended to condemn you, but to be a tool.

This book was written to demonstrate that what is impossible for man, through redemption, saving grace of Jesus Christ, and power in Jesus' name, the Son of God, all things can be made possible (Luke 18:27). You too can be redeemed from past decisions and mistakes; just like King David, Paul after his conversion from Saul to Paul, and the like. Don't you know Romans 8:28?

"And we know that all things work together for good to them that love God, to them who are called according to his purpose."

So how can you get back under the anointing? How can you get back to where you may have fallen? One must repentant and be sincere with seeking forgiveness. Don't allow yourself to be tricked into giving up your anointing, favor, and protection from God to chase the things of this world or man's approval.

King Saul had to learn what we all can read about today and avoid the fall. If we mess up, be like King David, and be quick to get in right standing with God. It is not to say there may not be a price to pay, but the Lord will be with you to go through whatever may come.

The Bible says perfect love castet out fear (1 John 4:18). Don't allow fear to chase you out of your divine right. Don't give your beauty for ashes. Be intentional, however, to press toward the mark and high calling of God. He then is faithful, to stand with you, to ensure you finish the race and He gets His glory.

A Prayer for the Lord's Restoration

I hereby issue a prophetic decree and a declaration of re-establishment in every sphere of your life. May the Lord, bring you to the rightful place, as commanded by him.

Moreover, any form of the broken crown in your business, relationships, marriage, career, ministry, children, healing, deliverance, miracle and destiny is fully restored in the Name of Jesus.

Blessed art thou,
Shalom!

Remember, You can choose not to withdraw from life, but rather to open your eyes to the lessons of life and be prepared to learn."

PROFILE OF BISHOP K.B. RANSFORD

INTRODUCTION

Bishop K.B. Ransford is a spiritual son of Bishop E.A.T. Sackey, Senior Associate with Bishop Dag Heward-Mills (founder of Lighthouse Chapel International). Bishop K.B., as popularly known, is the founder and the presiding Bishop of Salvation Prayer Mission World-Wide (SPMWW) which began in a home setting 20 years ago in South Africa.

His ministry is distinguished by a strong atmosphere of God's presence that is usually accompanied by signs, miracles, and wonders, and the way the Lord often opens his eyes to people's lives, circumstances and situations. SPMWW has gained both local and international divine recognition through this calling of God over his life as an apostolic prophetic revivalist.

His office has granted him international exposure in ministering intensively across Europe and Africa in Crusades, Conferences, and in church planting as well. The ministry has planted branches in South Africa and Ghana with its main headquarters based in Tshatshu, King William's Town, South Africa. Below is a brief description of his input in areas and initiatives he has established or participated in:

i. GENERAL IMPACTS THE GREAT COMMISSION

Bishop has raised, trained, and ordained pastors, evangelists, and leaders. Despite that, he remains part of various initiatives that promote and manifest the great commission of

Christ. One such initiative is the Annual Oil of Greatness Conference, which targets equipping and imparting into leaders of different denominations.

One Day Prayer Answered is another annual non-denominational gathering spearheaded by the Bishop to gather pastors, leaders, and souls to engage in the power of corporate prayer.

In 2016 Bishop was privileged to be the chairperson of a team of local pastors tasked to organize the massive Healing Jesus Crusade (King Williams Town). The campaign whose President is Bishop Dag Heward-Mills saw hundreds of souls accepting Christ to the Glory of God.

ii. COMMUNITY BUILDING

Bishop K.B. caters to the needy, the sick, orphans, widows and prisoners. Together with his team of leaders, he reaches out to people in various complex situations to the glory of God. In various initiatives to communities, prisons, schools, hospitals, Bishop K.B. has been a beacon of hope. As such; God granted him an honour to be invited by the former Executive Mayor, her lordship,

Ms. Zukiswa Ncitha, as a guest speaker at the State Adresss of the 2014 Buffalo City Municipality.

iii. SCHOOLS

He founded the Discovery of Gifts Ministries International (DGMI) that deals with churches, pastors, leaders, ordinations, and affiliations. DGMI is a non-denominational network in discovering the gifts and callings within the body of Christ.

He also established the Dominion Bible Institute that is a non-denominational school of ministry that trains and equips end-time generals in the Kingdom of God.

iv. AUTHOR

He has authored various writings like, Why do people fall under the anointing? Children's Prayer Book, this book (The Big mistake of Saul) and other church material.

v. PROPHETIC AIRWAVES

Further influences on the spiritual development and ministry of Bishop K.B. Ransford came from The Prophetic Voice which was broadcasted on TBN in Eastern

Cape Province in South Africa.

vi. INTERNATIONAL RECOGNITION AWARD

God being so faithful, in January 2020 Bishop received a prestigious award of Global Ambassador of Human Rights and Peace by the International Human Rights Advisory Council (IHRAC) based in India. This kind of award is awarded to people whose contribution to humanity is commendable.

Currently, Bishop is ministering on Rainbow Radio International which can be tuned to the program of the church, *the TRAD point*. Anyone from around the world can tune in on the following platforms:

Ghana FM 87.5 FM

UK London – DAB

UK Manchester – DAB Plus

Europe – Eurobird and Astra Television

Around the globe – Alexa box

Rainbow Radio online and Facebook

Monday to Friday from 21:30 to 22:00,

South Africa time.

Connect with K.B. Ransford

Facebook: Bishop KB Ransford

Twitter: @Bishop_ kb

LinkedIn: Bishop KB Ransford

Audio Podcast (Castbox): Please search for KB Ransford

Anchor: Bishop KB Ransford

CHURCH OFFICE

Salvation Prayer Mission World Wide

The Miracle Centre, Tshatshu

King William's Town

Eastern Cape Province

SOUTH AFRICA

Email: salvationprayermission@gmail.com

Telephone numbers:

+ 27 73 041-5183

+27 73199-0562

www.ingramcontent.com/pod-product-compliance
Lightning Source LLC
Chambersburg PA
CBHW030846090426
42737CB00009B/1120